THE HEART OF MAN

12 BIBLE STUDIES ABOUT THE SPIRITUAL CONDITION OF THE HUMAN HEART

TEACHER'S EDITION

Pastor Jeremy Markle

Walking in the WORD Ministries
Pastor Jeremy Markle
www.walkinginthewordministries.net

THE HEART OF MAN

12 BIBLE STUDIES
ABOUT THE SPIRITUAL CONDITION
OF THE HUMAN HEART

TEACHER'S EDITION

All rights reserved solely by the author.
No part of this book may be reproduced, stored in a retrieval system, or transmitted in any form or by any means– electronic, mechanical, photocopy, recording, or otherwise– without written permission of the author.

Unless otherwise noted,
all Scripture quotations are from the King James Version.

Second Edition
Copyright © 2019 by Pastor Jeremy Markle.
First edition published in 2017.

Published by Walking in the WORD Ministries
www.walkinginthewordministries.net

Printed in the United States of America

ISBN: 978-1947430280

CONTENT

SECTION 1

THE CLEANSING OF THE HEART

Lesson 1 - The Wickedness of a Man's Heart .. 7
Lesson 2 - The Worth of a Man's Heart 17
Lesson 3 - The Weeping of a Man's Heart 27
Lesson 4 - The Washing of a Man's Heart 39

SECTION 2

THE GROWING OF THE HEART

Lesson 1 - The Walking of a Man's Heart 47
Lesson 2 - The Willingness of a Man's Heart .. 55
Lesson 3 - The Weaning of a Man's Heart 63
Lesson 4 - The Worshiping of a Man's Heart .. 73

SECTION 3

THE WAYWARDNESS OF THE HEART

Lesson 1 - The Weakening of a Man's Heart .. 83
Lesson 2 - The Wandering of a Man's Heart .. 93
Lesson 3 - The Whipping of a Man's Heart ... 101
Lesson 4 - The Worrying of a Man's Heart ... 107

SECTION 1

THE CLEANSING OF THE HEART

Lesson 1
The Wickedness of a Man's Heart
(Man's Sin)

Lesson 2
The Worth of a Man's Heart
(God's Payment for Man's Sin)

Lesson 3
The Weeping of a Man's Heart
(Repentance for Salvation)

Lesson 4
The Washing of a Man's Heart
(Confession & Forgiveness)

Psalm 51:7, 10, 12
*Purge me with hyssop, and I shall be clean:
wash me, and I shall be whiter than snow.
Create in me a clean heart, O God;
and renew a right spirit within me.
Restore unto me the joy of thy salvation;
and uphold me with thy free spirit.*

Lesson 1

The Wickedness of a Man's Heart

The Wickedness of a Man's Heart
(Man's Sin)

The wickedness of man's heart began at the very beginning of time. For it was in the garden of Eden that man chose to serve self and seek selfish pleasure. In Genesis chapter 3, we find the source of all mankind's wickedness and pride. When Eve *"saw that the tree was good for food, and that it was pleasant to the eyes, and a tree to be desired to make one wise, she took of the fruit thereof, and did eat, and gave also unto her husband with her; and he did eat"* (Genesis 3:6). The very beginning of man's sinfulness was conceived in the perfect environment of God's creation, but was sourced in mankind's desire to fulfill personal desires. How wicked mankind is to rebel against the God who has created, preserved, and loved him (I John 2:15-17)! *(Question # 1)*

Do not jump so quickly to judge Adam and Eve before you take into account your own life. The Bible says, *"For all have sinned, and come short of the glory of God"* (Romans 3:23, I John 3:4). And Isaiah 53:6 says, *"All we like sheep have gone astray; we have turned every one to his own way ..."* The Bible is clear, each person has chosen to rebel against God. And how wicked and vile man really is! He has rudely turned his back to the face of his own Creator and chosen to follow self. *(Questions # 2, 3)*

Make no mistake, if man is to have fellowship with his Creator, he must be perfect like his Creator (I Peter 1:15-16, I John 1:5-8). In Psalm 5:4-6, King David said, *"For thou art not a God that hath pleasure in wickedness: neither shall evil dwell with thee. The foolish shall not stand in thy sight: thou hatest all workers of iniquity. Thou shalt destroy them that speak leasing: the LORD will abhor the bloody and deceitful man."* Because of mankind's fall from his created perfection, God has had to separate himself from mankind. And, sinful man is required to pay the penalty of his sin, which is death (Romans 6:23). *(Questions # 4, 5)*

The Heart of Man
The Wickedness of a Man's Heart

Nothing man does can ever make him perfect. Even man's attempt to do right ends in sin according to Isaiah 64:6, which says, *"But we are all as unclean, and all our righteousness are as filthy rags; and we all do fade as a leaf; and our iniquities, like the wind, have taken us away."* Consider the simple list of the Ten Commandments God gave the Israelites to obey. Have you kept them perfectly? Can you go through one day without breaking, at the very least, one of them? According to James 2:10, *"whosoever shall keep the whole law, and yet offend in one point, he is guilty of all."* This is not referring to just one day of your life, it is referring to your entire life. Can you honestly say that you have never sinned one single time in your whole life? I John 1:8 says, *"If we [you] say that we [you] have no sin, we [you] deceive ourselves [yourself], and the truth is not in us [you]."* According to Psalm 58:3, even children *"go astray as soon as they be born, speaking lies."* *"For all have sinned, and come short of the glory of God"* (Romans 3:23). Each one of us must come to the conclusion that we cannot meet God's level of perfection because we are sinners and God is holy (Jeremiah 17:9-10). *(Questions # 6, 7, 8)*

God has demanded holiness, and mankind has failed. Oh, how wretched we are! Man has no choice but to cry out as the prophet Isaiah did when he said, *"Then said I, Woe is me! for I am undone; because I am a man of unclean lips, and I dwell in the midst of a people of unclean lips ..."* (Isaiah 6:5). Isaiah did not stop at expressing the truth concerning his wickedness, but he also found a solution to that wickedness through the forgiving and cleansing power of God. Isaiah 6:6-7 says, *"Then flew one of the seraphims unto me, having a live coal in his hand, which he had taken with the tongs from off the altar: And he laid it upon my mouth, and said, Lo, this hath touched thy lips; and thine iniquity is taken away, and thy sin purged."* You can also have your sin taken away if you will have faith in Jesus Christ alone (John 3:15-17, Romans 10:9-10, Ephesians 2:8-9, Philippians 3:4-9, I John 1:9, I Corinthians 15:1-4). *(Questions # 9, 10, 11)*

The Heart of Man
The Wickedness of a Man's Heart

Romans 3:23
*For all have sinned,
and come short of the glory of God;*

Romans 6:23
*For the wages of sin is death;
but the gift of God is eternal life
through Jesus Christ our Lord.*

The Heart of Man
The Wickedness of a Man's Heart

Review Questions

1. Genesis 3:1-6 (6), I John 2:15-17 - How was Eve's temptation similar to the three sources of temptation given in I John 2:15-7?
   Lust of the flesh - <u>Saw that the tree was good for food</u>
   Lust of the eyes - <u>That it was pleasant to the eyes</u>

   Pride of life - <u>A tree to be desired to make one wise</u>

2. Romans 3:23 - Who has given in to temptation and has sinned? <u>Everyone</u>
   I John 3:4 - What is sin? <u>The transgression of the law</u>
   Have you ever committed a sin? _____

3. Isaiah 53:6 - Have you ever done your will rather than obeying God? _____

4. I Peter 1:15-16, I John 5:5-8, Psalm 5:4-6 - Can God have fellowship with a sinner? <u>No</u>

The Heart of Man
The Wickedness of a Man's Heart

5. Romans 6:23 - If you earn $400 per week from your employer for the 40 hours you have worked, we would consider that your wages or what you deserve. What do you deserve because of your life of sin according to the Bible? **Death**

6. Isaiah 64:6 - Name the best "GOOD WORK" you have ever done. _____

   Compared to God's holiness, what is that "GOOD WORK"? **Filthy rags**
   How good do you have to be in order to be equal with God? **Perfect**

7. James 2:10 - How much of God's perfect law are you guilty of violating? **All of it**

8. I John 1:8, Psalms 58:3, Romans 3:23 - Have you ever sinned? **Yes**

9. Isaiah 6:5 - Are you a sinner? **Yes**
   Have you ever sinned with your mouth? **Yes**
   (Also see Jeremias 17:9-10)

10. Isaiah 6:6-7 - Are you interested in God's cleansing for your sins? _____

    *If have answered yes to answer #10, follow through with answering #11.

The Heart of Man
The Wickedness of a Man's Heart

11. John 3:15-18, Ephesians 2:8-9, Philippians 3:4-9, I John 1:9 - You must have faith alone in Jesus Christ's death, burial, and resurrection as the only payment for your sins in order to receive God's forgiveness and eternal life (I Corinthians 15:1-4). Will you accept God's free gift right now by simply telling God you are trusting Him alone? Your statement of trust must be meant from the heart and not just words from your mouth (Romans 10:9-10).

If you have told God that you want His cleansing, why not write down your request to Him on the next page.

Dear God,

_____
_____
_____
_____
_____
_____
_____
_____
_____
_____
_____
_____
_____
_____

The Heart of Man
The Wickedness of a Man's Heart

Lesson 2

The Worth of a Man's Heart
(God's Payment for Man's Sin)

  The value of an object can be determined by two different value systems. The first system is focused on the object itself. For example, an object that is new, shiny or apparently of good quality may be worth a great deal of money, whereas an object that is old, dull, or of low quality may be worth much less. This value system can lead to a great deal of over-priced or under-priced objects because it is simply basing its worth upon appearance. This type of system is used by a used car dealer. A buyer is not so inclined to purchase an old, dull, and low quality car, therefore the salesman may take an old car and wash it or even give it a new paint job, just to make the sale. He knows that an average buyer has many other options and that his car must look good or he will never make the sale, because for the most part, the sale is simply based on how the car appears. However, the true value of a car is based on its reliability for transportation. Because the average buyer cannot determine the true value, he can only base his opinion upon the outward appearance.

  If God were to use this value system to determine whether He would purchase a man from the slave market of sin, that man would never be bought. As we saw in the previous lesson, "The Wickedness of Man's Heart," man is worthless and vile (Jeremiah 17:9-10, I Samuel 16:7). Just as you would not wish to pay any price for an old, dull, and low quality car, so God, based upon this process of decision making, would not wish to pay any price for an old, dull, or low quality man. Because no man would wish to waste his money on junk, we would have to come to the conclusion that based upon this value system, man is worthless. Praise God, He does not use this system of value and decision making, but rather He adds an additional figure to the value system equation, which is found in the second value system. *(Question # 1)*

  The second value system is focused more on the buyer than on the object being bought. The equation of value is changed to contain "desire." It is desire which changes an

The Heart of Man
The Worth of a Man's Heart

average buyer of an average car into an interested buyer of a specific car. This system of value can be illustrated by an auction. At an auction, one may find old, rickety, and seemingly useless objects which are sold for a great deal of money. These objects are not valuable in themselves, but for their novelty (for sometimes they are very old). But, because the buyer sees value in something and wishes to have it, he is willing to pay any price necessary to become the owner of that object. This value system is the system which God uses to determine man's value. God desires that *"all men to be saved, and to come unto the knowledge of the truth"* (I Timothy 2:4, II Peter 3:9), so He offered the highest price possible to ensure that all those who accept His payment will become His own precious possessions (I Corinthians 6:20, 7:23, Philippians 2:5-8, I John 4:9-10). Because this value system is based upon the buyer, the object could be of no actual value, and yet the given price would be quite high because value is based upon the actual price paid for the object. Let us take a look at how much God values each of His created beings (Luke 12:6-7, 22-32). *(Questions # 2, 3, 4)*

Jeremiah 17:9-10 says, *"the heart is deceitful above all things, and desperately wicked: who can know it?"* (Isaiah 64:6-7). No man could ever claim he deserves the death of another man, for every man is wicked and without worth (Romans 5:6-8, Ephesians 2:1-5, 8-9). But God, because of His love, paid a price which exceeds this world's goods (I Peter 1:18-21). Romans 5:6-8 says, *"For when we were yet without strength, in due time Christ died for the ungodly. For scarcely for a righteous man will one die: yet peradventure for a good man some would even dare to die. But God commendeth his love toward us, in that, while we were yet sinners, Christ died for us."* God sent His Son Jesus Christ to pay for man's sin-sick soul with His own blood because of His love for man (John 3:16, Romans 5:8-10, II Corinthians 5:21, Hebrews 9:22, 26-28). *(Questions # 5, 6, 7)*

Based on God's value system, every individual is worth the blood of Jesus (I John 2:1-2, 4:9-10). Because God has placed

The Heart of Man
The Worth of a Man's Heart

a great value upon each one of us. Will you accept His value system and payment for you and your sin? If you refuse, you are refusing the greatest gift ever given: God Himself! Oh, how wonderful to recognize that God loved me that much (Romans 5:8, Ephesians 2:1-5)! God has invited everyone to accept His gift of salvation. He is not partial or prejudiced (Matthew 28:18-20, Romans 10:12-13, Revelation 5:9), but He is particular. You must come to the Father through the Son (John 14:6-7, I Timothy 2:3-6). He is particular in that you must trust Him alone for your salvation (Ephesians 2:8-9). God's gift of salvation is offered to every one (John 3:16, Romans 6:23). God is *"not willing that any should perish, but that all should come to repentance"* (II Peter 3:9, Hebrews 9:24-28). *(Questions # 8, 9, 10, 11, 12, 13, 14)*

I John 4:9-10
In this was manifested the love of God toward us,
because that God sent his only begotten Son into the world,
that we might live through him.
Herein is love, not that we loved God,
but that he loved us,
and sent his Son to be the propitiation for our sins.

The Heart of Man
The Worth of a Man's Heart

Review Questions

1. Jeremiah 17:9-10 - Is your heart naturally good or wicked? Wicked
I Samuel 16:7 - What does God look at when He judges you? My heart

2. I Timothy 2:4, II Peter 3:9 - Who does God want to accept Him as their Savior so that He can pay for their debt of sin? Everyone

3. I Corinthians 6:20, 7:23, Philippians 2:5-8, I John 4:9-10 - What price did God pay for you to be freed from sin's penalty? Jesus Christ - His only begotten Son

4. Luke 12:6-7, 22-32 - Does God consider your life valuable? Yes

5. Isaiah 64:6-7, Jeremiah 17:9-10, Romans 5:6-12, Ephesians 2:1-5, 8-9 - Are you good enough to pay for your own sin debt by:
    Doing good deeds? No
    Going to church? No
    Helping the sick? No

6. John 3:15-18, Romans 5:6-10, II Corinthians 5:21 - Who is able to and has already paid for your sin debt? Jesus Christ

The Heart of Man
The Worth of a Man's Heart

7. I Peter 1:18-21, Hebrews 9:14, 22, 26-28 - What price did Jesus Christ pay in order to set you free from sin? <u>His blood</u>

8. I John 2:1-2, 4:9-10 - For whom has the blood of Jesus Christ paid? <u>Everyone</u>

9. Romans 5:8, Ephesians 2:1-5 - In what condition were you when Christ died for you? <u>A sinner</u>

10. Matthew 28:18-20, Romans 10:12-13 - Is God prejudiced against anyone? <u>No</u>
    Revelation 5:9 - Who is in heaven following salvation?
         Every <u>kindred</u>
         Every <u>tongue</u>
         Every <u>people</u>
         Every <u>nation</u>

11. John 14:6-7, I Timothy 2:3-6 - Who is the only source of salvation? <u>Jesus Christ</u>

12. Ephesians 2:8-9
    8 For by <u>grace</u> are ye saved through <u>faith</u>; and that Not of <u>yourselves</u>: it is a <u>gift</u> of God: 9 Not of <u>works</u>, lest any <u>man</u> should <u>boast</u>.

The Heart of Man
The Worth of a Man's Heart

13. John 3:16, Romans 6:23 - Have you accepted God's gift of eternal life through Jesus Christ's death, burial, and resurrection? _____

14. II Peter 3:9, Hebrews 9:24-28 - God wants everyone to be saved from eternal separation from Him and hell! If you could not answer yes to question #12, why not accept Jesus Christ's payment for your sins right now? _____

Acts 2:21b - "*...That whosoever shall call on the name of the Lord shall be saved.*"

Lesson 3

The Weeping of a Man's Heart

The Weeping of a Man's Heart
(Repentance for Salvation)

Scripture clearly teaches that man's heart is full of wickedness (Jeremiah 17:9-10, Ephesians 2:1-3), and that only because of God's personal love for man, He paid the price for that wickedness so that man dose not have to spend all eternity in hell (Romans 5:6-8, Ephesians 2:1-9, I John 4:9-10, I Corinthians 15:1-9, I Peter 2:21-25). Because of God's gift of love, man should be full of relief and joy (John 10:10). However, before that joy can come, and before that freedom can be experienced there must be weeping or repentance (Psalms 51:1-4, Acts 3:19, II Corinthians 7:9-11). This weeping is produced by the realization of man's rebellion and sin against the Holy, Righteous and Loving God (Isaiah 6:1-5). This weeping or repenting must be rooted in man's soul, and not just an outward appearance of emotions. For example, in Psalm 32:1-5 and Psalm 51:1-12, David wept because of his guilt from his sins and begged God for mercy. He said, *"Have mercy upon me, O God, according to thy lovingkindness: according unto the multitude of thy tender mercies blot out my transgressions. Wash me throughly from mine iniquity, and cleanse me from my sin. For I acknowledge my transgressions: and my sin is ever before me. Against thee, thee only, have I sinned, and done this evil in thy sight: that thou mightest be justified when thou speakest, and be clear when thou judgest"* (Psalm 51:1-4). So a sinner must come to terms with the reality of his wickedness, thus resulting in total and complete brokeness of spirit. *(Questions # 1, 2, 3, 4, 5, 6, 7)*

Often times, weeping is related to an emotional outburst, an expression of great sorrow in an individual's thoughts, emotions, and life. Although this form of weeping may be part of the process of getting right with God, it is not the root of spiritual sorrow. A weeping needed more than an outward display of sorrow is the spiritual weeping. True spiritual weeping is repentance and says, *"I acknowledge my sin unto thee, and mine iniquity have I not hid. I said, I will confess my transgressions unto the Lord; and thou forgavest the iniquity of*

The Heart of Man
The Weeping of a Man's Heart

my sin" (Psalms 32:5, I John 1:8-9). This repentance can only come from a man realizing his unworthiness and God's greatness, and must continue in the recognition that a great price was paid for his wicked soul by God Himself through Christ Jesus. (Question # 8)

Luke 7:36-50 gives an example of an outward weeping rooted in a spiritual realization and appreciation for Christ. Here a wicked women washed Christ's feet with perfume, tears, and her own hair, all because she recognized that Christ was her only source of salvation. She expressed the repentace of her heart in a public display. However, the display was not the most important aspect of this women's life. Rather, she recognized Jesus Christ as her Savior. She was willing to give her all to Him in worship because she realized that it was through Him that her lost condition was resolved.

Acts 16:22-34 provides a second example of a spiritual weeping. In this account, a jailor, who had kept Paul prisoner, falls under the conviction of the Holy Spirit. The jailor's reaction to God's conviction is seen when he fell to his face and said, *"what must I do to be saved?"* (Acts 16:30). Please notice that Paul's immediate response was, *"Believe on the Lord Jesus Christ, and thou shalt be saved, and thy house"* (Acts 16:31). This man's need of salvation could not be satisfied by Paul's power, but rather through the acceptance of Christ as his personal Savior (Romans 8:1, 10:13). Have you repented over your great sin against God and asked Him to forgive you?

The joy of the Lord is experienced after the weeping of repentance is completed (Psalms 51:12, Romans 15:13, II Corinthians 7:9-10). The joy found in salvation is sourced in the promise of forgiveness of sin and a home in heaven with God for all eternity (I John 5:13, Romans 8:18). *(Questions # 9, 10)*

The Heart of Man
The Weeping of a Man's Heart

II Peter 3:9
The Lord is not slack concerning his promise,
as some men count slackness;
but is longsuffering to us-ward,
not willing that any should perish,
but that all should come to repentance.

The Heart of Man
The Weeping of a Man's Heart

Review Questions

1. Jeremiah 17:9-10, Ephesians 2:1-3 - What is the condition of an unsaved individual? <u>Dead in trespasses and sins</u>

2. Romans 5:6-8, I John 4:9-10 - Who has paid the penalty for sin? <u>Jesus Christ</u>

3. I Corinthians 15:1-4, I Peter 2:21-25 - What did Jesus have to do to pay for your sin? <u>Die on the cross</u>

4. John 10:10 - What type of life does God want you to have? <u>Abundant</u>

5. Psalms 51:1-4, Acts 3:19, II Corinthians 7:9-11 - What should be the cause of your sorrow before you can experience the joy of salvation? <u>My sin</u>
   *What type of sorrow should you have? <u>Heavenly</u>

6. Isaiah 6:1-5, Psalms 51:1-4 - Have you recognized your sinful condition? _____
(Also see Luke 7:36-50, Acts 16:22-34)

The Heart of Man
The Weeping of a Man's Heart

7. Psalms 32:1-5, 51:1-12 - Have you **asked** God for forgiveness of your sinful condition? _____

8. Psalms 32:5, I John 1:8-9 - Have you **accepted in full** God's forgiveness of your sin? _____ (Also see Romans 8:1, 10:13)

9. Psalms 51:12, II Corinthians 7:9-10, Romans 15:13, I John 5:13 - If you are assured of your salvation, do you have the joy that comes from knowing your eternal destiny because of your salvation? _____

10. Romans 8:18 - ***For I reckon that the sufferings of this present time are not worthy to be compared with the glory which shall be revealed in us.***

WARNING!

GO NO FURTHER WITHOUT CAREFUL CONSIDERATION!

A Time to Reflect

Before you continue any further, I invite you to reflect upon the last three lessons. Have you understood them? Do you have any questions about what was said? If you do, please, immediately contact your pastor or the individual who is sharing these lessons with you, and present your questions to them so that you might have a clear understanding of Christ's gift of salvation for you.

If you do not have any questions and you have not accepted Christ as your Savior yet, why not do so today (Proverbs 27:1, II Corinthians 6:2)? It is as simple as agreeing with God and believing in God. First, do you agree that you are a sinner (Romans 3:23)? Second, do you agree that your sin will send you to hell (Romans 6:23)? Third, do you believe that God has loved you so much that He sent His Son to die for your sins (John 3:14-17) and that He is the only source of your personal salvation (Romans 3:23-28)? Will you accept God's free gift of salvation personally by simply trusting in Christ's death on the cross as the only solution to your sin and eternal destiny of hell (Romans 5:6-10)?

Romans 10:9-13

That if thou shalt confess with thy mouth the Lord Jesus,
and shalt believe in thine heart that God
hath raised him from the dead,
thou shalt be saved.
For with the heart man believeth unto righteousness;
and with the mouth confession is made unto salvation.
For the scripture saith,
Whosoever believeth on him shall not be ashamed.
For there is no difference between the Jew and the Greek:
for the same Lord over all is rich unto all that call upon him.
For whosoever shall call upon the name of the Lord
shall be saved.

Lesson 4

The Washing of a Man's Heart

The Washing of a Man's Heart
(Confession & Forgiveness)

In the process of everyday life, everyone becomes dirty and in need of a physical washing. The medical industry has recognized the importance of cleanliness and recognizes that a dirty wound that is full of infectious germs must be purified before it can heal properly.

The spiritual life is no different in reference to cleanliness. If you have completed the previous lessons, you will recall that man is wicked, dirty, and vile (Jeremiah 17:9-10, Romans 3:10-18, 23). You will also remember that Christ paid for your wickedness on the cross, and all you must do to partake of His payment is trust in Him alone (Romans 10:9-10, Ephesians 2:8-9). If you have accepted Christ as your Savior, you have received the cleansing of your sins from your life. Isaiah 1:18 illustrates this biblical truth by stating, *"come now, and let us reason together, saith the LORD: though your sins be as scarlet, they shall be as white as snow; though they be red like crimson, they shall be as wool"* (Psalms 51:1-12). In II Corinthians 5:17, the apostle Paul allows us to understand an even greater truth. He says about salvation: *"Therefore if any man be in Christ, he is a new creature: old things are passed away; behold, all things are become new"* (II Corinthians 5:17-21). *(Questions # 1, 2, 3, 4)*

God does not want you to continue to carry the dirt of this world while you walk through life (Romans 6:1-2, Titus 2:11-14). Therefore, God not only provides the forgiveness for your sin at salvation, but I John 1:9 gives you the assurance that you can come to God every time you sin, by saying, *"If we confess our sins, he is faithful and just to forgive us our sins, and to cleanse us from all unrighteousness."* The same blood of Christ that saved you from death and hell has the power to pay for your daily sins (Romans 6:11-18). In order to receive forgiveness for your sin, simply confess them to God. Confession is agreeing with God that the wrongdoing is truly sin and was committed against Him (II Corinthians 7:9-10). God promises you His faithfulness and His justice every time you confess your sins. Based on God's faithfulness and justice, you can be assured that God will forgive you and never hold a grudge. But that He has removed your sins *"as far as the east is from the west ..."* (Psalms 103:8-12). *(Questions # 5, 6, 7, 8, 9, 10)*

I John 1:9
If we confess our sins,
he is faithful and just to forgive us our sins,
and to cleanse us from all unrighteousness.

The Heart of Man
The Washing of a Man's Heart

Review Questions

1. Jeremiah 17:9-10, Romans 3:10-18, 23 - Were you spiritually righteous or unrighteous before your salvation? Unrighteous

2. Ephesians 2:8-9, Romans 10:9-10 - How did you receive salvation through Jesus Christ? By faith

3. Isaiah 1:18, Psalms 51:1-12 - What did your sin look like before you accepted Christ as your Savior? Scarlet, red like crimson
What did your sin look like after you accepted Christ as your savior? White as snow, like wool

4. II Corinthians 5:17-21 - What does it mean to be made new? To have anew standing with God in a new spiritual relationship with Him as well as have anew purpose for living

5. Romans 6:1-23 (1-2, 15), Titus 2:11-14 - Does God want you to sin constantly because you know that He will forgive you? No

6. I John 1:9 - Does God have the power to forgive you of your sin even after salvation? Yes
What does God promise you if you will confess your sins to him? Cleansing and forgiveness

The Heart of Man
The Washing of a Man's Heart

7. Romans 6:11-18 - Who can help you overcome your sin in your Christian life? <u>God</u>

8. II Corinthians 7:9-10 - What does godly repentance (sorrow) produce? <u>Life</u>
What does worldly repentance (sorrow) produce? <u>Death</u>

9. Psalms 103:8-12 - How far does God remove your sins from you, if you confess them to Him? <u>As far as the East from the West</u>

**Are there sins
which you should ask forgiveness for right now?**

SECTION 2

THE GROWING OF THE HEART

Lesson 1
The Walking of a Man's Heart
(Obeying God / The Life of Faith)

Lesson 2
The Willingness of a Man's Heart
(Baptism & Church Membership)

Lesson 3
The Weaning of a Man's Heart
(Spiritual Maturity)

Lesson 4
The Worshiping of a Man's Heart
(Glorifying God)

Psalm 51:7, 10, 12
*Purge me with hyssop, and I shall be clean:
wash me, and I shall be whiter than snow.
Create in me a clean heart, O God;
and renew a right spirit within me.
Restore unto me the joy of thy salvation;
and uphold me with thy free spirit.*

Lesson 1

The Walking of a Man's Heart

The Walking of a Man's Heart
(Obedience to God / The Life of Faith)

Men and women have been walking on planned paths since the beginning of time. It is only by the work of individuals like Daniel Boon, who marked paths through the frontier, that our own nation has expanded and progressed. Physical trails are important for the traveler to arrive safely at his proper destination.

This same principle is used when talking of an individual's SPIRITUAL WALK. Each believer must decide what path he wishes to follow. We are warned in Matthew 7:13-14, *"enter ye in at the strait gate: for wide is the gate, and broad is the way, that leadeth to destruction, and many there be which go in thereat: because strait is the gate, and narrow is the way, which leadeth unto life, and few there be that find"* (John 10:7-10, 14:6-7). Each believer has already decided to enter through the narrow gate of faith when he accepted Christ as his personal Savior and only way of salvation. But even believers can be distracted from the narrow path of faith, which may seem hard and lonely (I Timothy 4:1, Proverbs 4:23-27, Ephesians 5:15-16). Because of the difficulty of this path, some believers will be distracted from the straight path and turn down side paths which seem easier, but lead to destruction (Hebrews 11:25, Proverbs 14:12, James 1:12-15, Genesis 2:16-17). How much better for a believer to heed the apostle Paul's encouragement to Timothy when he said, *"Fight the good fight of faith ..."* (I Timothy 6:12, Ephesians 6:10-18). Please recognize that after you have entered the gate of faith for salvation you can never lose your salvation (I John 5:13), but you can be distracted from a proper Christian life if you begin to love the things of the world (II Timothy 4:10, I John 2:15-17). *(Questions # 1,2,3,4,5,6)*

The Apostle Paul used the illustration of a runner in a race to explain how he was staying focused and completing his spiritual life to the honor and glory of God (I Corinthians 9:24-27). As a believer, you must also stay focused on your destination, which is being conformed to the image of Jesus

The Heart of Man
The Walking of a Man's Heart

Christ (Romans 8:28-29, Philippians 2:5-7, II Timothy 4:7-8). *(Questions # 7,8)*

Hebrews 11 presents a number of faithful individuals who experienced God's strength because of their faith. Hebrews 12:1-3 follows this list by saying, *"Wherefore seeing we also are compassed about with so great a cloud of witnesses, let us lay aside every weight, and the sin which doth so easily beset us, and let us run with patience the race that is set before us, Looking unto Jesus the author and finisher of our faith; who for the joy that was set before him endured the cross, despising the shame, and is set down a the right hand of the throne of God. For consider him that endured such contradiction of sinners against himself, lest ye be wearied and faint in your mind."* *(Question # 9)*

Are you willing to commit yourself to live by faith according to the Word of God (Habakkuk 4:2, Romans 10:17, II Corinthians 5:7)? Are you going to walk through your spiritual life trusting God rather than your own abilities (Hebrews 11:1, 6)? *(Questions # 10,11,12)*

*A book you could read which might encourage you in your Christian walk is *Pilgrim's Progress* by John Bunyan.

II Corinthians 5:7
(For we walk by faith, not by sight:)

The Heart of Man
The Walking of a Man's Heart

Review Questions

1. Matthew 7:13-14 - Describe the way which leads to destruction. <u>Wide and broad</u>
How many people will go the way to destruction? <u>Many</u>
Describe the way which leads to life. <u>Strait and narrow</u>
How many people will go the way to life? <u>Few</u>

2. I Timothy 4:1 - What does God say will take place in the *"latter times?"* <u>Some shall depart from the faith</u>
Proverbs 4:23-27 - How should you live so that you are not distracted from the right way? <u>Carefully, Straight</u>
(Also see Ephesians 5:15-16)

3. Hebrews 11:25 - How long does sin seem fun? <u>For a season</u>
Proverbs 14:12 - What takes place when man follows his own thoughts? <u>Death</u>
James 1:12-15 - What is the result of sin? <u>Death</u>
(Also see Genesis 2:16-17)

4. I Timothy 6:12 - What fight must you fight? <u>The good fight of faith</u>
(Also see Ephesians 6:10-18)

The Heart of Man
The Walking of a Man's Heart

5. I John 5:13 - Does God want you to know for sure you have a home in heaven? <u>Yes</u>

6. II Timothy 4:10, I John 2:15-17 - What are you warned against? <u>The love of the world</u>

7. I Corinthians 9:24-27 - Why did Paul wish to stay faithful to God in his Christian walk and ministry? <u>Lest ... I myself should be a castaway</u>

8. Romans 8:28-29 - Whose image does God want you to look like? <u>God the Son (Jesus Christ)</u>
(Also see Philippians 2:5-7)
II Timothy 4:7-8 - What is the reward of keeping the "faith?" <u>A crown of righteousness</u>

9. Hebrews 12:1-3 - Who is the *"author and finisher of our faith?"* <u>Jesus Christ</u>
What encouragements does this passage give you personally for your life of faith? _____
_____

10. Habakkuk 2:4a - How does a wicked/unjust person live? <u>In pride - lifted up</u>
Habakkuk 2:4b, II Corinthians 5:7 - How does a righteous/just person live? <u>By faith</u>
(Romans 10:17 - True faith is always based on the teaching of God's Word.)

The Heart of Man
The Walking of a Man's Heart

11. Hebrews 11:1 - Is it faith to see and understand all of life's circumstances? <u>No</u>

12. Hebrews 11:6
6 But without <u>faith</u> it is impossible to <u>please</u> him: for he that <u>cometh</u> to <u>God</u> must <u>believe</u> that he is, and that he is a <u>rewarder</u> of them that <u>diligently</u> <u>seek</u> him.

Lesson 2

The **Willingness** of a **Man's Heart**

The Willingness of a Man's Heart
(Baptism & Church Membership)

God has directed men and women to obey Him in many different ways throughout history. Examples of those who have been willing to obey Him are found in Hebrews chapter 11. Some of these faithful individuals suffered a great deal because of their obedience, yet God commends them because their obedience showed their faith in Him (James 2:17-20, John 14:15). *(Question # 1)*

According to the book of Acts, those who trusted in Jesus Christ as their personal Savior followed their conversion with two specific steps of obedience to tell the entire world that they had become a follower of Jesus Christ.

First, new believers were baptized immediately after their salvation (Acts 2:37-47, 8:27-40). Also, a command was given to all believers from Jesus Christ to *"Go ye therefore, and teach all nations, baptizing them in the name of the Father, and of the Son, and of the Holy Ghost: Teaching them to observe all things whatsoever I have commanded you: and, lo, I am with you alway, even unto the end of the world"* (Matthew 28:18-20). This command is given to all believers to show, first, the importance of salvation through Christ alone to the lost world and, second, to show those who accept Christ as Savior that they must now tell the whole world that they are following Jesus Christ. Baptism does not have any saving power, for Jesus Christ did not need salvation but was baptized to signify that He was obedient to God the Father and separated from the world (Matthew 3:13-17). Followers of Jesus Christ must be baptized following their salvation to signify that they are separated from the world unto Jesus Christ (Romans 6:1-15, II Corinthians 6:14-18, James 4:8, I Peter 2:11-12). Are you willing to show others around you that you have trusted Jesus as your Savior? Are you willing to testify to others that you identify with Jesus' death, burial and resurrection to pay for your sin and your eternal destiny? *(Questions # 2, 3, 4)*

The Heart of Man
The Willingness of a Man's Heart

Second, we find in Acts that after baptism believers were added unto the (local) church (Acts 2:41). The way we express that today is to say that they "joined the church." God has designated that from the time of Jesus Christ's resurrection until His return the local church is to be a believer's source of encouragement and teaching about God and the Christian life (Hebrews 10:23-25). God has also designated that the leadership of the church is to be teaching believers how to do the *"work of the ministry"* (Ephesians 4:11-16). Also, in Titus chapter 2, God instructs all those who have become spiritually mature to teach and help those who are younger. As you can see, God has a special reason for having new believers join with a local church. *(Questions # 6, 7, 8, 9)*

Are you willing to obey God by joining a local church, which will help you learn about God and encourage you to live a godly life (James 4:17)? *(Question # 10)*

James 4:17
Therefore to him that knoweth to do good, and doeth it not, to him it is sin.

The Heart of Man
The Willingness of a Man's Heart

Review Questions

1. James 2:17-20 - What is an evidence of true faith? <u>Good works</u>
   John 14:15 - What is an expression of true love? <u>Obedience</u>

2. Acts 2:37-47 - What did the new believers do soon after being saved? <u>Immediately</u>
   Acts 8:26-40 - What did Philip tell the Ethiopian eunuch he must do before he could be baptized? <u>Believe</u>
   On whom did the eunuch believe? <u>Jesus Christ</u>
   Did Philip and the eunuch **go into** the water? <u>Yes</u>

3. Matthew 28:18-20 - In Whose name are believers baptized? <u>God the Father, the Son (Jesus Christ), and the Holy Spirit</u>

4. Matthew 3:13-17 - With Whom are believers identifying when they are baptized? <u>Jesus Christ</u>

5. Romans 6:1-15, II Corinthians 6:14-18, James 4:8, I Peter 2:11-12 - From what are you to separate? <u>Sin - world - flesh</u>
   To whom are you to be separated unto? <u>God</u>

The Heart of Man
The Willingness of a Man's Heart

6. Acts 2:41 - What two things took place before the people were added unto the church?
   a. Received the Word - Believe in Jesus Christ
   b. Baptized

7. Hebrews 10:23-25 - Are you to gather/fellowship with fellow believers? Yes
   Why do believers gather/fellowship together?
    To provoke unto love and to good works

8. Ephesians 4:11-12 - What is the job of church leadership?
   a. *The **perfecting** [maturing] the saints*
      1. *For the **work** of the ministry*
      2. *For the **edifying** of the body of Christ*

9. Ephesians 4:13-16 - What are the benefits of being in a local church?
   a. Verse 13
      1. *Till we all come in the **unity** of the faith*
      2. *Till we all come in the unity ... of the **knowledge** of the Son of God*
      3. *Till we all come ... unto a **perfect** [mature] man, unto the measure of the stature of the fulness of Christ*

The Heart of Man
The Willingness of a Man's Heart

    b. Verse 14
        1. *That we henceforth be no more <u>children</u>, tossed to and fro, and carried about with every wind of doctrine, by the sleight of men, and cunning craftiness, whereby they lie in wait to deceive*
    c. Verse 15
        1. *But <u>speaking</u> the truth in love*
        2. *May <u>grow</u> up into him in all things, which is the head, even Chris:*
    d. Verse 16
        1. *From whom the whole body fitly <u>joined</u> together and <u>compacted</u> by that which every joint supplieth*
        2. *According to the effectual <u>working</u> in the measure of every part*
        3. *Maketh increase of the body unto the <u>edifying</u> of itself in love*

10. James 4:17 - What should you change or do in your life according to this verse? _____

Lesson 3

The Weaning of a Man's Heart

The Weaning of a Man's Heart
(Spiritual Maturity)

As a newborn baby physically must gain nourishment from its mother's milk, so a new convert must turn to the simple truths of scripture to find spiritual milk for his new life in Christ (I Peter 2:1-3). The new believer must be introduced to and apply these truths to his life or he will always maintain the spiritual level of an infant (I Corinthians 3:1-2, Hebrews 5:11-14). *(Questions # 1, 2)*

The first truth a new believer must be introduced to through Bible study is the caring and greatness of our God (II Peter 1:2-4). It is God Who created him (Psalms 22:10-11, John 1:3), it is God Who keeps him (Psalms 121), it is God Who loves him (I John 4:15-19), and it is God Who takes care of his every need and concern (Psalms 103, Matthew 6:25-34). *(Questions # 3, 4, 5, 6, 7)*

Second, a new believer must be introduced to the importance of a continual study of God's Word, the Bible (II Timothy 3:16-17). It is only through this Book, and the study of it, that he will ever grow in his spiritual life (Psalms 1:1-6, 119:9-11, I Peter 2:1-3,). *(Question # 8)*

Third, a new believer must be introduced to the importance of prayer. Through prayer a believer finds fellowship and communication with God, forgiveness of sin, and comfort, and strength in times of need (Matthew 6:5-15, Philippians 4:6-7, Hebrews 4:14-16, James 4:2-3, Psalms 37:4-5). *(Questions # 9, 10, 11)*

Fourth, a new believer must be introduced to the importance of attending a good local church (Hebrews 10:23-25). It is the local church which God has ordained to help and encourage a believer to grow to maturity (Ephesians 4:11-16, Hebrews 13:7, 17). *(Questions # 12, 13, 14)*

Fifth, a new believer needs to understand that he is a new creature in Christ and that he does not follow the world's way of living or thinking (II Corinthians 5:17-21, Romans 6). He must understand that *"no man can serve two masters: for either he*

The Heart of Man
The Weaning of a Man's Heart

will hate the one, and love the other; or else he will hold to the one, and despise the other. Ye can not serve God and mammon" (Matthew 6:24, I John 2:15-17). *(Questions #15, 16)*

As a new believer begins to understand God through the simple truths of scripture, and applies those truths to his life, he can be introduced to deeper studies that are prompted by personal interests and his life circumstances. Studies expanded by books, word studies, subject studies, etc. can be used to deepen his knowledge of God and the Christian life. These deeper studies can be very helpful and maturing, but a new believer must be cautious to not overwhelm himself or confuse himself (II Timothy 2:15). In order to avoid confusion, he must be careful to allow the Spirit of God to guide him (John 16:13) through prayer (Matthew 7:7-8, James 1:5-8) and verse-by-verse Bible reading (Psalms 119:9, 11, II Timothy 3:16-17). He can also seek the help of other spiritual leaders, such as pastors, deacons, teachers, etc. (Ephesians 4:11-16, Titus 2). *(Questions #17, 18, 19, 20, 21)*

Are you participating in these five steps to spiritual growth?

I Timothy 3:16-17
All scripture is given by inspiration of God,
and is profitable for doctrine,
for reproof,
for correction,
for instruction in righteousness:
That the man of God may be perfect,
throughly furnished unto all good works.

The Heart of Man
The Weaning of a Man's Heart

Review Questions

1. I Peter 2:1-3 - What is the result of drinking spiritual milk, the Bible? <u>Growth</u>

2. I Corinthians 3:1-2, Hebrews 11:14 - What are you if you do not grow from eating spiritual milk to spiritual meat? <u>Carnal</u>

3. II Peter 1:2-4
   2 <u>Grace</u> and <u>peace</u> be multiplied unto you through the <u>knowledge</u> of God, and of Jesus our Lord,
   3 According as his divine power hath <u>given</u> unto us <u>all</u> things that pertain unto <u>life</u> and <u>godliness</u>, through the <u>knowledge</u> of him that hath called us to glory and virtue:
   4 Whereby are given unto us exceeding great and precious <u>promises</u>: that by these ye might be partakers of the <u>divine</u> nature, having escaped the <u>corruption</u> that is in the world through lust.

4. Psalms 22:10-11, John 1:3 - Who has made you and given you life? <u>God</u>

5. Psalms 121 - Who is sustaining you? <u>God</u>

6. I John 4:15-19 - Who loved first, God or man? <u>God</u>

The Heart of Man
The Weaning of a Man's Heart

7. Psalms 103 - Make a short list of some of the blessings you have received by being one of God's children.
   a. _____
   b. _____
   c. _____
   d. _____
   Matthew 6:25-34 - Who will take care of your needs, if you will trust Him? God

8. II Timothy 3:16-17 - Name the four things for which God's Word is used.
   a. Doctrine - Teaching what is correct
   b. Reproof - Finding what is incorrect
   c. Correction - Fixing what is incorrect
   d. Instruction - Preventing of what is incorrect
   (Also see Psalms 1:1-6, 119:9-11, I Peter 2:1-3)
   What will result in your spiritual life if you read and apply God's Word? Be perfect ... all good works

The Heart of Man
The Weaning of a Man's Heart

9. Matthew 6:5-15 - Name key truths taught about prayer from this passage.
   a. Verses 5-6 - <u>Pray in secret (privet)</u>
   b. Verses 7-8 - <u>Don't use vain repetition</u>
   c. Verses 9-15 - For what things did Jesus pray?
      i. <u>God's name to be sanctified</u>
      ii. <u>God's kingdom to come</u>
      iii. <u>God's will to be done</u>
      iv. <u>Daily bread to be provided</u>
      v. <u>Forgive sin</u>
      vi. <u>Protect from temptation and evil</u>

10. Philippians 4:6-7 - For what should you pray? <u>All things</u>
    What is the result from giving your requests to God? <u>Peace that passes understanding</u>
    (Also see Hebrews 4:14-16)

11. James 4:2 - Why do you not have what you desire? <u>We do not ask</u>
    James 4:3 - Why do you not have what you ask for? <u>We are selfish</u>
    Psalms 37:4-5 - What is the key to receiving what you ask for? <u>Delighting in God</u>

12. Hebrews 10:23-25 - What did some begin to do that they should not have done? <u>Forsake church</u>

13. Ephesians 4:11-16 - (Review Section 2, Lesion 2, questions 6 & 7)

The Heart of Man
The Weaning of a Man's Heart

14. Hebrews 13:7, 17 - How should you respond to spiritual leadership?
    a. Remember them
    b. Follow their faith
    c. Consider the end of their conversation
    d. Obey them
    e. Submit to them

15. II Corinthians 5:17
    17 Therefore if any man be in <u>Christ</u>, he is a <u>new</u> creature: <u>old</u> things are <u>passed</u> away; behold, <u>all</u> things are become <u>new</u>.
    (Also see II Corinthians 5:17-21, Romans 6)

16. Matthew 6:24, I John 2:15-17 - There is a saying which goes:
    "Only two choices on the shelf,
    Pleasing God or pleasing self."
    What choice are you going to make? _____

17. II Timothy 2:15 - Is there any shame in studying God's Word? No

18. John 16:13 - What does the Holy Spirit guide you to know? Truth

The Heart of Man
The Weaning of a Man's Heart

19. Matthew 7:7-8, James 1:5-8 - What does God promise you if you ...
    Ask - _Receive_
    Seek - _Find_
    Knock - _Opened_

20. Psalms 119:9 - What do you need to use to help clean your spiritual life? _The Bible_
    Psalms 119:11 - What must you do with the Bible to help prevent you from sin? _Hide (memorize) it_
    II Timothy 2:15 - What command is given to you about the Bible in this verse? _Rightly divide (study) it_

21. Ephesians 4:11-16, Titus 2 - Does God use other believers to help you grow spiritually? _Yes_

Lesson 4

The **Worshiping** of a Man's Heart

The Worshiping of a Man's Heart
(Glorifying God)

A maturing believer must recognize that his main purpose for being on the earth is not to make his home here (Hebrews 11:13, I Peter 2:11), but rather to give praise and glory to God (Colossians 3:16-17, Psalms 9, 18:1-3, 34:1-3, 148). Worshiping God goes far beyond just singing songs and listening to sermons at church (Ephesians 3:21, I Peter 5:10-11, I Corinthians 10:31). The process of worshiping God is carried out every time a believer is showing God His due respect, obedience, and glory (praise) (Psalms 29:1-2). *(Questions # 1, 2, 3)*

A believer must first recognize who God is. He is the *"King of kings and Lord of lords"* (I Timothy 6:14-16, Revelation 19:11-16). God must be the designated King of a believer's life in order for a him to properly worship God (Deuteronomy 5:7-9, Exodus 20:3-5). *(Questions # 4, 5)*

Second, a believer must find God as His Lord and Master. No man can serve two masters (Matthew 6:24, I John 2:15-17). Even the apostle Paul did not consider himself to be free following his salvation, but rather he considered himself a "prisoner" of Christ (Ephesians 4:1, Philemon 1:1). A servant does not question his master's commands or requests. A servant (bond slave) looks to please and obey only one person: his master. I Corinthians 10:31 clearly teaches that a believer is to give God glory in everything he does (I Corinthians 6:19-20). God also desires a believer to express his worship and praise through obedience more than in religious ceremony (I Samuel 15:22-23). If you have truly taken the first step of making God King, the second step of making God Master should become easy and natural. *(Questions # 6, 7, 8, 9)*

Third, a believer's worship of God does include praise and an outward expression of what God has done for him. The Psalms command, us to *"make a joyful noise unto the Lord, all ye lands"* (Psalms 100, 103). God gave Israel a special song they were to learn in order to remind them of God's greatness and their need for Him (Deuteronomy 31:19-21, 30, 32:1-47, Ephesians

The Heart of Man
The Worshiping of a Man's Heart

5:19-20). Luke 19:37-40 says that if Jesus Christ would not have received proper praise, the rocks would have cried out. Paul and Silas are a good example of those who praised God in a vocal and musical way, even while they were under great persecution, because their hearts were in tune with God (Matthew 12:34-37). While in pain, these two servants of God praised Him for his love and tender care (Acts 16:19-26, James 1:2-4). *(Questions # 10, 11, 12, 13, 14)*

It is possible that you are going through hard times and your life is seemingly filled with misery. For you, the subject of praise may need to be simply rooted in your salvation and faith that God still loves you and is providing for you even though you may not understand or see the provision (Romans 8:17-18). You must also look toward the promise from God that He will one day eliminate all pain and sorrow (Revelation 21:4). *(Question # 15)*

Worshiping God can be done through every aspect of life by simply respecting, obeying, and praising God (Psalms 95:1-11, Romans 12:1-2). These things are necessary to live an abundant Christian life (John 10:10). *(Questions # 16, 17, 18)*

I Corinthians 10:31
Whether therefore ye eat,
or drink, or whatsoever ye do,
do all to the glory of God.

The Heart of Man
The Worshiping of a Man's Heart

Review Questions

1. Hebrews 11:13, I Peter 2:11 - What are you to be on this earth? <u>A stranger and pilgrim</u>

2. Colossians 3:16-17, Psalms 9, 18:1-3, 148 - What are you encouraged to do continually with the Word of God? <u>Let it dwell abundantly in my life Lord</u>

3. Ephesians 3:21, I Peter 5:10-11 - Who is supposed to receive glory from the church? <u>Jesus Christ</u>
I Corinthians 10:31 - When are you to do things to God's glory? <u>Always</u>
(Also see Psalms 29:1-2)

4. I Timothy 6:14-16, Revelation 19:11-16 - What does it mean to be a King of kings and Lord of lords? <u>To have total authority and receive all the glory</u>

5. Deuteronomy 5:7-9, Exodus 20:3-5 - Are you to serve any other god? <u>No</u>

6. Matthew 6:24, I John 2:15-17 - How many masters can you serve? <u>One</u>
Which master will you choose? _____

The Heart of Man
The Worshiping of a Man's Heart

7. Ephesians 4:1, Philemon 1:1 - Are you willing to be a prisoner of Jesus Christ? Paul counted it a privilege! _____

8. I Corinthians 6:19-20, 10:31 - Who should receive glory from your life? God the Father and Jesus Christ

9. I Samuel 15:22-23 - What is better, your sacrifice or obedience? Obedience

10. Psalms 100, 103 - How should you express your praise to God? By singing

11. Ephesians 5:19-20 - What should you sing to remind you of God? Songs, Hymns, and Spiritual Songs
(Also see Deuteronomy 31:19-21, 30, 32:1-47)

12. Luke 19:37-40 - What does Jesus say would have taken place if He did not receive His proper praise? The stones would immediately cry out _____

13. Matthew 12:34-37 - What does your speech reveal about your heart? If it is good or evil

14. Acts 16:19-26, James 1:2-4 - Are you willing to praise God even in tough times? _____

The Heart of Man
The Worshiping of a Man's Heart

15. Romans 8:17-18 - Are you dwelling more on your future in heaven or on the trials of today? _____

    (Also see Revelation 21:4)

16. Psalms 95:1-11
    1 O come, let us <u>sing</u> unto the LORD: let us make a <u>joyful</u> noise to the rock of our salvation.
    2 Let us come before his presence with <u>thanksgiving</u>, and make a <u>joyful</u> noise unto him with psalms.
    3 For the LORD is a great <u>God</u>, and a great <u>King</u> above all gods.
    4 In his hand are the deep places of the earth: the strength of the hills is his also.
    5 The sea is his, and he made it: and his hands formed the dry land.
    6 O come, let us <u>worship</u> and <u>bow</u> <u>down</u>: let us <u>kneel</u> before the LORD our maker.
    7 For he is our <u>God</u>; and we are the <u>people</u> of his pasture, and the sheep of his hand. To day if ye will hear his voice,

17. Romans 12:1-2 - What is your reasonable service for God? <u>Living sacrificially and holy for Him according to His will</u>

18. John 10:10 - What type of life does God wish you to have? <u>Abundant</u>

SECTION 3

THE WAYWARDNESS OF THE HEART

Lesson 1
The Weakening of a Man's Heart
(Spiritual Forgetfulness)

Lesson 2
The Wandering of a Man's Heart
(Temptation)

Lesson 3
The Whipping of a Man's Heart
(Conviction & Correction)

Lesson 4
The Worrying of a Man's Heart
(Eternal Security)

Psalm 51:7, 10, 12
Purge me with hyssop, and I shall be clean:
wash me, and I shall be whiter than snow.
Create in me a clean heart, O God;
and renew a right spirit within me.
Restore unto me the joy of thy salvation;
and uphold me with thy free spirit.

Lesson 1

The Weakening of a Man's Heart

The Weakening of a Man's Heart
(Spiritual Forgetfulness)

Mankind is constantly forgetting things. For example, we forget where we put our keys, if we paid the phone bill, or we might accidentally forget to take out the garbage. As humans, we are subject to forgetfulness. This forgetfulness can cause major or minor problems with those around us. But how major is the problem of forgetting the One Who created, saved, and personally cares for each of us? In Deuteronomy 8:2-3,11-20 Moses instructs the Israelite people to constantly remember who God is and what He had done, for if they forgot, they would wander away to other gods, and therefore punished by God. How important it is that a believer remember the God Who created, saved and cares for Him. If he fears God, insomuch that he remembers His presence and His holiness, he will never wander from His commandments (Psalms 111:10). *(Questions # 1, 2)*

The process of weakening our spiritual life begins with forgetting God and not using the power given by God to conquer sin (Romans 6:1-6, 15-22, I Corinthians 10:12-13, Titus 2:11-14). Forgetting God leads a believer to forget those things which keep him in touch with God and to neglect the spiritual tools God has given to him (Ephesians 6:10-20). For example, some of the forgotten necessities of a faithful Christian life are the spiritual food of God's Word (II Timothy 3:16-17), the spiritual communication of prayer (Philippians 4:6-7, James 4:1-3), a continual, personal evaluation of one's sin and confession of that sin (Psalms 32, 51, 119:9-11, 139:23-24, James 1:22-25, Hebrews 4:12, I John 1:9, 2:1-2), and the spiritual fellowship and accountability of the local church (Hebrews 10:23-25, Ephesians 4:11-16). *(Questions # 3, 4, 5, 6, 7, 8)*

God gives a believer no excuse for forgetfulness. He has warned each believer to not never forget the wonderful work of salvation that He had accomplished to save him from his sin and old life (Ephesians 2:1-10, II Peter 1:5-15). And for that wonderful work of salvation, God deserves the believers constant attention and glory (I Corinthians 6:19-20, 10:31). Only by

The Heart of Man
The Weakening of a Man's Heart

specifically remembering his Lord, Savior, God, Master, King, etc., can he ever keep his heart in tune with God. When a believer forgets God and his personal pride takes over (Proverbs 3:5-8, 16:18) that he is "*... drawn away by his [our] own lusts and enticed ...*" (James 1:12-15). *(Questions # 9, 10, 11, 12)*

In James 1:19-25, God has given a two step protective process by which you can be assured not to forget Him and His commandments. First, James 1:19-21 presents a clear indication that you must be a listener to the "*engrafted word, which is able to save your souls.*" You must constantly be confronted with the truths of Scripture and not give more value to your personal opinions. You must humbly listen to God as He guides and directs (Psalms 31:1-3, 32:7-8, 143:10). Second, James 1:22-24 says, "*But be ye doers of the word, and not hearers only, deceiving your own selves. For if any be a hearer of the word, and not a doer, he is like a man beholding his natural face in a glass: for he beholdeth himself, and goeth his way, and straightway forgetteth what manner of man he was.*" How damaging it would be if after you listened to God's Word, you forgot to follow it and fail to make adjustments to your life based upon it! How much spiritual sleep is in your eyes, or how disheveled is your spiritual hair? God promises in James 1:25 that, "*But whoso looketh into the perfect law of liberty, and continueth therein, he being not a forgetful hearer, but a doer of the work, this man shall be blessed in his deed.*" *(Questions # 13, 14, 15, 16)*

Have you started to become weak in your spiritual walk? Have you forgotten all that God has done for you and the power over sin you have through Him (Romans 6:6-18)? Have you stopped listening to God and His Word? Have you forgotten to do the things you have heard? If so, will you repent of your sin? God promises you His forgiveness, for He desires you to have a right relationship with Him at all times (Hebrews 12:4-11, I John 1:9). *(Questions # 17, 18)*

The Heart of Man
The Weakening of a Man's Heart

James 22-25
But be ye doers of the word, and not hearers only,
deceiving your own selves.
For if any be a hearer of the word, and not a doer,
he is like unto a man beholding his natural face in a glass:
For he beholdeth himself, and goeth his way,
and straightway forgetteth what manner of man he was.
But whoso looketh into the perfect law of liberty,
and continueth therein, he being not a forgetful hearer,
but a doer of the work, this man shall be blessed in his deed.

The Heart of Man
The Weakening of a Man's Heart

Review Questions

1. Deuteronomy 8:2, 11-20 (11, 18-20) - What must you do to prevent you from sinning? <u>Remember your God, His provision, and His instruction</u>

2. Psalms 111:10 - What are the blessing that come from fearing and obeying God?
10 The fear of the LORD is the beginning of <u>wisdom</u>: a good <u>understanding</u> have all they that do his commandments: his <u>praise</u> endureth for ever.

3. Romans 6:1-6, 15-22, I Corinthians 10:12-13 - Does God want you to continue sinning after you are saved? <u>No</u>
Does God give you the power to combat sin? <u>Yes</u>
(Also see Titus 2:11-14)

The Heart of Man
The Weakening of a Man's Heart

4. Ephesians 6:10-20 - What are the pieces of the spiritual armor believers are to put on?
   a. Verse 14 - **Loins girt about with <u>truth</u>**
   b. Verse 14 - **Breastplate of <u>righteousness</u>**
   c. Verse 15 - **Feet shod with the preparation of the <u>gospel</u> of <u>peace</u>**
   d. Verse 16 - **Shield of <u>faith</u>**
   e. Verse 17 - **Helmet of <u>salvation</u>**
   f. Verse 17 - **Sword of the Spirit, which is the <u>Word</u> of <u>God</u>**
   With what are you to always use these pieces of armor? (Verses 18-20) <u>Prayer</u>

5. II Timothy 3:16-17- Why should you be constantly reading God's Word? <u>So that I am by perfect (mature) and fully ready able to do good works</u>

6. Philippians 4:6-7, I Thessalonians 5:17-18, James 4:1-3 - What Does God command you commanded to do constantly? <u>Pray</u>

7. James 1:22-25 - What spiritual object is illustrated by a mirror and should be used to help you see your sin? <u>God's Word</u>
   (Also see Psalms 119:9-11, 139:23-24, Hebrews 4:12)
   I John 1:9, 2:1-2 - What does God provide when you ask For forgiveness? <u>Cleansing</u>
   (Also see Psalms 32, 51)

The Heart of Man
The Weakening of a Man's Heart

8. Hebrews 10:23-25 - Why should you be faithful in attending the church?
   23 Let us <u>hold</u> fast the profession of our <u>faith</u> without wavering; (for he is faithful that promised;)
   *24 And let us consider one another to <u>provoke</u> unto <u>love</u> and to good **works**:*
   25 Not forsaking the assembling of ourselves together, as the manner of some is; but <u>exhorting</u> one another: and so much the more, as ye see the day approaching.
   (Also see Ephesians 4:11-16)

9. Ephesians 2:1-10, II Peter 1:5-15 - What must you remember to prevent you from returning to your old life and sin? <u>My wonderful salvation from sin and the old life through the work of Jesus Christ</u>

10. I Corinthians 6:19-20, 10:31 - What are you to do to God's glory? <u>Everything</u>

11. Proverbs 3:5-8, 16:18 - What are you commanded not to follow? <u>My own wisdom</u>

12. James 1:12-15 - Whose lust draws you away from looking at God and then sinning? <u>My own</u>

13. James 1:19-21 - What are you to listen to in order to prevent temptation and sin from controlling your life? <u>The Bible / God's Word</u>

The Heart of Man
The Weakening of a Man's Heart

14. Psalms 31:1-3, 32:7-8, 143:10 - What should you constantly be seeking? God's leading

15. James 1:22-24 - After the Bible is heard, what must a you do with what you have heard? Be a doer

16. James 1:25 - What is the result of hearing and doing the Word of God? Blessing

17. Romans 6:6-18 - Are you freed from the power of sin? Yes
    Who has freed you from the power of sin? Jesus Christ

18. Hebrews 12:4-13 - What should God's chastening cause you to do? Produce fruit of righteousness

    I John 1:9 - What does God promise you if you will confess your known sins? Forgiveness and cleansing from all sin

Lesson 2

The Wandering of a Man's Heart

The Wandering of a Man's Heart
(Temptation)

A child of God who has forgotten Who God is and His salvation, will naturally begin to wander away from the purity God wishes him to have (II Peter 1:8-15, Deuteronomy 6:1-25). A believer is similar to a child who tries to steal a cookie from the cookie jar, forgetting that mom and dad are watching. If he would have remembered the presence and authority of his parents, he would never have tried to do something he knew would lead to punishment. Sin in the life of a believer comes from being distracted from God. James 1:13-15 presents a clear picture of the process leading to sin in the life of a believer.

James 1:13-15
*Let no Man say when he is tempted,
I am tempted of God:
for God cannot be tempted with evil,
neither tempteth He any man:
But every man is tempted,
when he is drawn away of his own lusts,
and enticed.
Then when lust hath conceived,
it bringeth forth sin:
and sin, when it is finished,
bringeth for death.*

Each believer must recognize that temptation does not come from God. God is holy and wishes His children to be holy (Leviticus 11:44, I Peter 1:13-16). Therefore, it goes against His nature to ever tempt a believer. *(Question # 1)*

According to Ephesians 2:1-3, temptation comes from three sources. This passage tells of man's sinful condition before salvation and gives the three main sources of sin and temptation. *"Wherein in time past ye walked according to the course of this world [world], according to the prince of the power of the air [Devil], the spirit that now worketh in the children of*

The Heart of Man
The Wandering of a Man's Heart

disobedience [flesh]: Among whom also we all had our conversation in times past in the lusts of the flesh, fulfilling the desires of the flesh and of the mind, and were by nature the children of wrath, even as others." (Question # 2)

Two of these sources are outside sources. The world, in reference to man's worldview or philosophy of living, is all around us and constantly presenting sin as fun and pleasureful. These temptations must be combated with God's warning that sin is only fun for a season (Hebrews 11:24). The Devil is also fighting against believers in order to destroy them (Ephesians 6:10-12, I Peter 5:8). The Devil wants nothing more than that each believer would destroy his life so that he can no longer be a bright light in this dark world (Matthew 5:13-16, II Corinthians 4:1-4). The world and the Devil work endlessly to distract believers from their focus on God. How much more of a determination to stay focused upon God do you need to have? *(Questions # 3, 4, 5)*

The third source of temptation is always present with a believer. He can never hide from it, and it will never leave him alone until he gets to heaven. This third source of temptation is our own sinful flesh. James 1:14 says *"But every man is tempted, when he is drawn away of his own lust, and enticed."* The starting point of temptation is personal lusts. Lust is a desire for anything that is outside of God's will. I John 2:16-17 speaks of three main wrongful desires that provide temptation opportunities when it says, *"For all that is in the world, the lust of the flesh, and the lust of the eyes, and the pride of life, is not of the Father, but is of the world. And the world passeth away, and the lust thereof: but he that doeth the will of God abideth for ever."* Temptation simply presents an ungodly desire in the believer's heart and mind and then teases him with it. Sometimes, the things he is tempted with are not bad, but are simply not God's will for his life at that time. For example, Jesus Christ was tempted by Satan while He was in the wilderness (Matthew 4:11). The first thing Satan used to tempt Jesus was

The Heart of Man
The Wandering of a Man's Heart

food. Eating is not sin, and Jesus was hungry, but the way Satan tempted Jesus to get the food was not according to God's will. Satan loves to present "good things" as temptation. Temptation must be dealt with quickly and firmly. Jesus Christ responded very confidently when He was tempted by Satan. He knew that His source of protection from temptation was the Word of God (Psalms 119:9, 11) and trust in His heavenly Father to do what was best (Ephesians 6:16). Jesus referred back to scripture in order to combat each of the temptations. Believers need to memorize and quote scripture to combat the temptation process which leads to sin. *(Questions # 6, 7, 8, 9)*

Please note that being tempted is not sin. Yielding to temptation is sin. Even Jesus Christ was tempted by Satan himself. Jesus's refusal to submit to temptation shows even more clearly that He is the perfect Son of God. Also, I Corinthians 10:13 gives you the assurance that God will not forget about you in your temptation, but rather is willing and able to help you conquer temptation(Hebrews 12:1-3, I John 5:3-5). *(Question # 10)*

I Corinthians 10:13
There hath no temptation taken you
but such as is common to man:
but God is faithful,
who will not suffer you to be tempted
above that ye are able;
but will with the temptation also make a way to escape,
that ye may be able to bear it.

The Heart of Man
The Wandering of a Man's Heart

Review Questions

1. II Peter 1:8-15 - You should remember that God saved you from what things? My old sins
(Also see Deuteronomy 6:1-25)

2. Leviticus 11:44, I Peter 1:13-16 - What does God command His children to be? Holy

3. Ephesians 2:1-3 - What are the three influences of sin and temptation?
   a. World (worldly culture)
   b. Devil (the prince of the air)
   c. Flesh (the spirit of disobedience)
   (Also see I John 2:15-17, Ephesians 6:11-12, I Peter 5:8, Romans 13:14, Galatians 5:16-26)

4. Hebrews 11:25 - How long does the fun of sin last? A season (a short time)

5. Ephesians 6:10-12, I Peter 5:8 - Who is seeking to destroy believers? The Devil

6. Matthew 5:14-16 - What are you to be in this dark world? A light
II Corinthians 4:1-4 - Can you be a light in this world if you are living like the world? No

The Heart of Man
The Wandering of a Man's Heart

7. James 1:14 - What draws you away from doing right? My own lusts

8. I John 2:16-17 - What are the three wrong desires (lusts) from the world?
   a. Lust of the flesh
   b. Lust of the eyes
   c. Pride fo Life

9. Matthew 4:1-11 - Write the three temptations of the Devil for Jesus with their category of worldly desires found in I John 2:16.
   a. Lust of the flesh - Turn a stone to bread
   b. Lust of the eyes - Jump from the temple and see God's protection
   c. Pride fo Life - Worship him to be king of all nations

10. Psalms 119:9, 11 - What must you do with God's Word in order to prevent sin in your life? Hide it in my heart (to remember it)

11. I Corinthians 10:13 - Will God allow you to be overwhelmed by temptation? No
    Does God help you with temptation if you will seek His help? Yes
    (Also see Hebrews 12:1-3, I John 5:3-5)

Lesson 4

The **Whipping** of a Man's Heart

The Whipping of a Man's Heart
(Conviction & Correction)

Just as a child must receive punishment for his disobedience to his parents, so must a believer receive corrective punishment from God. Hebrews 12:1-13 presents some great truths concerning the subject of sin and the chastening of God. Verses 1-4 encourage a believer to not forget all that God has done for him and to continue to *"be striving against sin."* The passage then goes on to describe the result of sin. Sin leads to death (James 1:14-15). God does not wish you to be burdened with the process or result of sin (Romans 6:1-2, 6-15, I Corinthians 15:55-58). For that reason, He may need to chasten you when you sin so that you do not continue to live in it's danger. *(Questions # 1, 2, 3, 4)*

God has set the standard for holiness, and because of His holiness, He cannot have any fellowship with sin (Habakkuk 1:13, I John 3:1-3). Psalm 66:18 says, *"If I regard iniquity in my heart, the Lord will hear me."* God does not wish for you to be constantly out of fellowship with Him, so He applies chastening to your life to help teach you how to keep fellowship with Him (John 14:15). *(Questions # 5, 6, 7)*

Hebrews 12:5 says, *"and ye have forgotten the exhortation which speaketh unto you as unto children, My son, despise not thou the chastening of the Lord, nor faint when thou art rebuked by Him."* God understands that *"now no chastening for the present seemeth to be joyous, but grievous"* (Hebrews 12:11a). He also recognizes man's need for correction. God's chastening is an expression of His love because He is attempting to teach the believer to stay close to Him (Hebrews 12:6). Man's wickedness drives him away from God's holiness, just as a child desires to play outside the protection of the fence. The safest place for the child is in the yard, and the safest place for a believer is in fellowship with God. Just as a parent must chasten his child when he tries to leave the yard, so God must chasten His children when they leave the safety of holiness (Hebrews 12:7-10). God's chastening should bring some comfort, for it is through His conviction and correction that you can know that you truly are part of His family. Hebrews 12:1-11 concludes with verses 12 and 13, which say, *"Wherefore lift up the hands which hang down, and the feeble knees; and make straight paths for your feet, lest that which is lame be turned out of the way; but let it rather be healed"* (Hebrews 12:12-13). God wants to show you that He loves you through His chastening and encourage you to heed His holiness, in order that those areas in your life that are weak spiritually can be healed and set back into their proper place of obedience. *(Questions # 8, 9, 10, 11)*

Hebrews 12:6, 11
For whom the Lord loveth he chasteneth,
and scourgeth every son whom he receiveth.
Now no chastening for the present seemeth to be joyous,
but grievous:
nevertheless afterward
it yieldeth the peaceable fruit of righteousness
unto them which are exercised thereby.

The Heart of Man
The Whipping of a Man's Heart

Review Questions

1. Read Hebrews 12:1-13.

2. Hebrews 12:1-4 - Why should you stay focused on Jesus Christ as the author and finisher of your faith?
   a. <u>To not be weary and faint</u>
   b. <u>To strive against sin</u>

3. James 1:14-15 - What is the result of sin? <u>Death (separation)</u>
   (Also see James 5:19-20, I John 5:16-17)

4. Romans 6:1-2, 6-15, I Corinthians 15:55-58 - Does God wish you to be a slave to sin after your salvation? <u>No</u>

5. I John 3:1-3 - What will you do if you are looking for the return of Jesus Christ? <u>Purify myself (live pure)</u>

6. Psalms 66:18, Habakkuk 1:13 - What places a barrier between you and God? <u>Sin, iniquity</u>

7. John 14:15 - What does your love for God produce? <u>Obedience</u>

The Heart of Man
The Whipping of a Man's Heart

8. Hebrews 12:5 - Does God wish to destroy you by chastening you? No

9. Hebrews 12:6 - What does God's chastening show you? His love

10. Hebrews 12:1-11 (10-11) - Why does God chasten you?
    a. To produce holiness
    b. To produce peaceable fruit of righteousness

11. Hebrews 12:12-13 - What does a proper understanding and heeding of God's chastening produce?
    a. Healing (restoration, encouragement)
    b. Straight paths (direction for life)

Lesson 4

The Worrying of a Man's Heart

The Worrying of a Man's Heart
(Eternal Security)

A young child who loves his mother and father may have doubts about his parents' love after he has disobeyed and is punished. A believer may face this same fear. God is his heavenly Father and if you love Him, you will want to please Him. When you fail to please God, you can become discouraged and question God's love (II Peter 1:1-10). As mentioned in the previous lesson, the conviction and chastening of God upon your life is proof of God's love for you. God does not wish you to be concerned that He would "disown" you. I John 4:16-19 clearly teaches that God's love can give you confidence in Him (Romans 8:31-39). There is no need for fear concerning the promise He has given to you about your eternal destiny. *(Questions # 1, 2)*

The God who loved you before you were saved is the same loving God who will keep you after your salvation. The assurance of your salvation and your security for all eternity must come from the same One Who forgave you of your sins at salvation (I Peter 1:3-5). Salvation is a gift from God and He is not an "Indian giver." I John 5:11-13 says, *"**And this is the record, that God hath given to us eternal life, and this life is in his Son. He that hath the Son hath life; and he that hath not the Son of God hath not life. These things have I written unto you that believe on the name of the Son of God; that ye may know that ye have eternal life, and that ye may believe on the name of the Son of God.**"* John 10:27-30 expresses very clearly that those who have trusted in Jesus Christ as their personal Savior will never be removed from His personal care. You are promised that you are "*... **sealed with that Holy Spirit of promise**"* (Ephesians 1:13-14, I Peter 1:3-5). The Holy Spirit could be illustrated as being the glue that holds you in God's hands. *(Questions # 3, 4)*

The forgiveness of God is not only present at the time of salvation, but continues throughout the rest of your life. I John 1:9 says, *"**if we confess our sins, he is faithful and just to forgive us our sins, and to cleanse us from all unrighteousness**"*

The Heart of Man
The Worrying of a Man's Heart

(Psalms 32, 51). Notice that if you confess your sins, God promises, upon His faithfulness and His justness, to forgive your sins. The verse also implies that if you confess your known sins, God will cleanse every sin you have committed, even if you didn't realize it. *(Question # 7)*

God's love continues for all times (Romans 8:36-39). After salvation, God does not wish you to continue in sin (Romans 6). When you do sin, you can turn to Him for forgiveness and as a good father would do for his child, God will openly and totally forgive the wrong you have done (I John 2:1-2). *(Questions # 8, 9, 10)*

I John 2:1-2
My little children,
these things write I unto you,
that ye sin not.
And if any man sin,
we have an advocate with the Father,
Jesus Christ the righteous:
And he is the propitiation for our sins:
and not for ours only,
but also for the sins of the whole world.

I John 5:12-13
He that hath the Son hath life;
and he that hath not the Son of God hath not life.
These things have I written unto you
that believe on the name of the Son of God;
that ye may know that ye have eternal life,
and that ye may believe on the name of the Son of God.

The Heart of Man
The Worrying of a Man's Heart

Review Questions

1. II Peter 1:1-10 - What should you add to your spiritual life? (5-7)
   Faith + <u>virtue</u> + <u>knowledge</u> + <u>temperance</u> + <u>patience</u> + <u>godliness</u> + <u>brotherly</u> <u>kindness</u> + <u>charity</u> = a fruitful Christian life
   What happens to those who do not strive to obey God and continue in sin? (8-9)
   a. *. . . be <u>barren</u> nor <u>unfruitful</u> in the knowledge of our Lord Jesus Christ.*
   b. *. . . is <u>blind</u>, and cannot see <u>afar</u> off, and hath <u>forgotten</u> that he was purged from his old sins.*

2. I John 4:16-19, Romans 8:31-39 - Is there any reason to fear losing God's love?   <u>No</u>

3. I Peter 1:3-5 - Who has given us the gift which is *". . . an inheritance incorruptible, and that fadeth not away, reserved in heaven for you?"*   <u>God</u>

4. I John 5:11-13 - If you have accepted Jesus Christ as your Savior, what do you have?   <u>Eternal life</u>
   Can you know that you have (eternal) life?   <u>Yes</u>

5. John 10:27-30 - Is there anything that can take you out of God's hands?   <u>No</u>

The Heart of Man
The Worrying of a Man's Heart

6. Ephesians 1:13-14, I Peter 1:3-5 - Who has sealed believers into the family of God? <u>The Holy Spirit</u>

7. I John 1:9 - Does God place a limit on when we can receive forgiveness from our sins? <u>No</u> (Psalms 32, 51)

8. Romans 8:36-39 - What will cause God to stop loving His children? <u>Nothing</u>

9. Romans 6 - Does God wish believers to rely on His grace to permit them to sin freely? <u>No</u>

10. I John 2:1-2 - Who is your source of forgiveness when you have sinned? <u>Jesus Christ</u>

II Timoteo 3:14-17
*But continue thou in the things which thou hast learned
and hast been assured of,
knowing of whom thou hast learned them;
And that from a child
thou hast known the holy scriptures,
which are able to make thee wise unto salvation
through faith which is in Christ Jesus.
All scripture is given by inspiration of God,
and is profitable for doctrine, for reproof,
for correction, for instruction in righteousness:
That the man of God may be perfect,
throughly furnished unto all good works.*

WILL YOU COMMIT YOUR LIFE TO GOD TODAY?

PLEASE DO NOT WASTE A MINUTE. YOU HAVE NO GUARANTEE OF TOMORROW.

Other Ministry Resources Available from Walking in the WORD Ministries

Marriage: A Covenant Before God presents 10 biblical studies about marriage, each one is based on the marital relationship of Adam and Eve and has the purpose of helping young couples understand God's plan and purpose for their life together. Included are practical questions, illustrations, and applications for each biblical truth in order that the couple might grow in their knowledge of each other and how they can glorify God together.

Parenting with Purpose seeks to help young parents to spiritually prepare for the great privilege they have to care for and guide the life of one of God's precious creations. The first three lessons focus on the parents' need to honor God with their child, while the final three lessons focus on the parents' opportunity to represent God the Father to their child.

The Armor of God for Your Daily Battles provides a daily Bible study to review the spiritual resources God has provided for each believer so that they can enjoy a victorious Christian life.

Walking in Newness of Life contains 13 chapters focusing on the privileges that each Christian can enjoy in his "new life" found in Jesus Christ, and the great promises that each of God's children can enjoy, as well as the great responsibilities he must fulfill as he walks "in newness of life" (Romans 6: 4).
*A study guide is available to be used personally or in a small group.

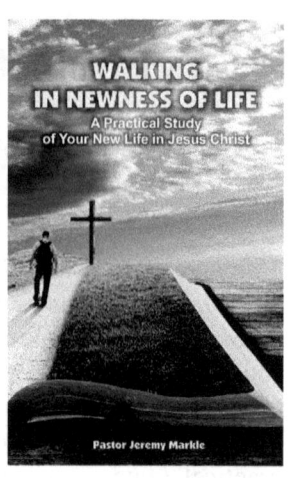

The Calvary Road: Outline Guide was written to enhance your ability to understand, remember, and apply the important spiritual truths shared by Roy Hession in his book, The Calvary Road. After reading each chapter, you can review its content by filling in the blanks, considering the additional passages provided, and answering the reflection and application questions. Throughout this outline guide there are a few special features to help you focus on the truths being taught.

We Would See Jesus: Outline Guide was written to enhance your ability to understand, remember, and apply the important spiritual truths shared by Roy Hession in his book, We Would See Jesus. After reading each chapter, you can review its content by filling in the blanks, considering the additional passages provided, and answering the reflection and application questions. Throughout this outline guide there are a few special features to help you focus on the truths being taught.

Your God Cares gives biblical hope in time of personal tragedy. It was written following the author's personal experience of living through a natural catastrophe and focuses on God's promise of love and concern for each of our difficulties no mater their size or significance to others. At the end of each chapter there are additional passages of Scripture to present God's promises for the reader's life.

Missions: Ministering Beyond Our Borders was written to provide insight into the physical, emotional, and spiritual adjustments a missionary faces as he begins his new life and ministry. Throughout its pages you will find spiritual encouragements for the missionary and helpful hints for his family and friends who desire to support him in his service to their Lord and Savior Jesus Christ. There is also a "Missionary Edition," which provides a large appendix with additional tips specifically for missionaries.

The Deputation Trail: Ministry or a Means to an End? was written to help missionaries during their pre-field ministry by presenting biblically-based philosophies and practical tips to guide them through a God-honoring, church-expanding, and believer-edifying, deputation ministry.

What Does the Bible Say About Salvation, Baptism, and Church Membership? provides a brief Biblical explanation for these three important subjects in the Christian life. Following each study are questions to help review each subject. These studies can be used with a new believer or pre-baptism or pre-church membership classes.

**Please visit
www.walkinginthewordministries.net
to find more biblical resources
in English and Spanish.**

www.ingramcontent.com/pod-product-compliance
Lightning Source LLC
Chambersburg PA
CBHW060519030426
42337CB00015B/1944